Original title:
Living Without Knowing Why

Copyright © 2025 Creative Arts Management OÜ
All rights reserved.

Author: Charles Whitfield
ISBN HARDBACK: 978-1-80566-191-7
ISBN PAPERBACK: 978-1-80566-486-4

The Art of Being Lost

I took a left and ended up right,
My map was a joke, quite a sight.
The GPS laughed, what a situation,
Turns out I was on a vacation!

Whispers of Uncertainty

The clock ticks loud, what is that sound?
A tick and a tock, I'm always spellbound.
Time's up, or is it? Where do I go?
Just follow the cat, it's part of the show!

Paths Without Signposts

I wandered in circles, round and round,
Like a washing machine, what've I found?
Each corner I turned, a surprise so grand,
Dancing with squirrels, that's my new plan!

The Enigma of Existence

Why is the sky blue? I'll never know,
Pondering fish is quite the show.
With thoughts like these, why worry or fret?
I'll ride on my bike, it's the best bet!

Beneath the Surface of Still Waters

Fish discuss their daily quests,
Chest full of seaweed, what a mess.
Bubbles pop with gossip abound,
Whale of a time without a sound.

Shadows glide, a curious dance,
Eels twirl around in a slimy trance.
The pond's a stage, yet none can see,
Why they sing with such glee and spree.

Echoes of Aimless Journeys

Wanderers roam without a clue,
Lost shoes, strange hats, and a sock or two.
Maps unfolded, but upside down,
"Are we in the right town or just a clown?"

Feet keep moving, hearts a-flutter,
Finding a snack is what matters utter.
Is that a mountain? Or just a hill?
Chasing shadows gives a thrill, oh what a thrill!

The Puzzle with Missing Pieces

Jigsaw chaos, pieces galore,
A corner where no edges score.
Assembling art? Or is it fate?
Left with the cat—she thinks it's great.

A blue one, maybe, or a red square,
Searching frantically everywhere.
Frustration's laugh, a silly chore,
Finding fun in the puzzle's war.

Stars Without Maps

Stars twinkle like disco lights,
But none are sure what night ignites.
"Which one is Colin? Or perhaps Sue?"
Naming them all, what a silly brew.

Planets wobble in cosmic spins,
Asteroids play, it's where the fun begins.
Chasing comets on a wild ride,
Navigating by gut—it's how they glide.

The Pulse of Indecision

In a world where choices sway,
I flip a coin for my day.
Some days I wear my socks askew,
While debating 'chicken' or 'beef stew.'

Should I dance or should I sit?
Potato chips, a wise choice, I admit.
But wait, there's cake on the shelf!
Deciding just to eat, not be myself!

A map I bought to find my way,
Yet, lost I am—hip hip hooray!
With every turn, a laugh I'd steer,
Oh look, it's Tuesday, not a fear!

Am I a sage or just naïve?
In each thought, I often grieve.
But life, it seems, is best when jester,
For joy finds us, our hearts, the tester.

Glimmers of the Unfathomable

Why did I walk into that wall?
Oh right, just to hear it call!
With every trip, I laugh and play,
Finding humor on this wobbly way.

The moon's my guide, I chat, I scream,
A rubber duck, my steadfast dream.
Yet, mystery hides in every grin,
Like why my toast lands butter-side in!

Glimpses of truth lurk behind a chair,
Like socks that vanish, I swear!
I chase the cat; it runs away,
Perhaps it knows what I can't say.

With winks and nods, we dance through light,
Juggling fate, what a silly sight!
In the swirl of the absurd, I find,
It's all a circus, fresh and blind.

Waiting for the Unrevealed

In a cafe, time's gone awry,
A fly's my date; I can't deny.
I sip my drink, an empty cup,
While staring at the ceiling up.

Why's the waiter slow as a snail?
I'd leap to fly, on a whim, I'd sail!
Still, here I ponder, mouth agape,
Waiting for life to change its shape.

A banner reads 'surprise inside,'
But here I sit, my joy's a slide.
The fridge hums tunes of lost delight,
As I wait for the unknown to bite.

Each second ticks, a quirky dance,
Like socks in dryers—will they prance?
I'll laugh 'til then, through this dull meal,
For what's to come, I must appeal!

Unspoken Echoes

In a vacant room where whispers rhyme,
I chat with shadows, passing time.
Each echo rolls like silly jokes,
While ghosts of thoughts parade like blokes.

A chair does creak; it says, 'Just sit.'
I ponder if it's talking fit.
What wisdom lies in silence here?
Or just the crumbs of a leftover beer?

Socks may shuffle in the night,
While I tie the wrong shoelace tight.
Yet in this mishmash of quirky lore,
I stand and dance by an unseen door.

So let the echoes hum and sway,
With laughter in the words we say.
For in this oddity, I feel at peace,
In the unspoken, my thoughts release.

Unseen Currents

In chaos we dance, with two left feet,
Juggling the joy of our self-made defeat.
We laugh at the fog, it thickens our plight,
With each step we take, we vanish from sight.

Questions like soap bubbles float through the air,
Popped by the laughter that hangs everywhere.
Why do we trip on what's hidden from view?
Oh, it's just part of the circus we do!

The Twilight of Clarity

In the twilight where ideas start to collide,
We wade through the mystery with flap and slide.
The answers elude, like a cat after prey,
While we chase our tails, in a comical fray.

With each pondered thought, we fumble and slip,
Like peas on a plate, take a dive and a dip.
What's the point anyway? Giggles abound,
As we tumble through life, on this merry-go-round.

Searching in the Depths

Diving down deep in a pool of lost dreams,
Where reality's logic unravels at seams.
We swim with confusion, a splash and a glee,
Like fish with no fins, we're just silly and free.

Bubbles of whims float to the top of the mind,
Popping in laughter, each one is a find.
Why is the sky blue? Who gave it a name?
In this game of bewilderment, we're all just the same.

The Path of Soft Questions

On the path where the questions are fluffy and round,
We bounce like a ball, with no answers found.
What's that over there? Oh wait, it's a breeze,
Tickling our senses, it aims to please.

As we wander and ponder, with glee in our stride,
We embrace every twist, on this laughable ride.
The world may seem strange, but we chuckle and play,
For the fun is the journey, come what may!

Footsteps in the Fog

In shoes too big, I wander far,
Tripping on clouds, beneath a star.
The path is here, but where's the guide?
I giggle loud, embracing the ride.

Each turn I take, it's a new surprise,
With shadows dancing, I squint my eyes.
A catwalk of giggles in a misty space,
I'm lost but smiling, at this silly race.

Dreams Adrift in Time

A clock is ticking, but what's the hour?
I'd bake a cake, but forgot the flour.
The dreams I chase are floating balloons,
I'm holding on, to comic tunes.

A time machine with broken wheels,
It rolls to lunch and steals my meals.
"Why?" I ask as I eat my cake,
The answer's vague, but oh, for goodness' sake!

The Canvas of Uncertainty

With brushes all crooked, I paint the air,
Splatters of logic, like a wild fair.
Each stroke a giggle, each color a dare,
Under splashes of "Where the heck's that hair?"

My canvas is fuzzy, a jumbled glee,
A masterpiece made of 'what could be.'
In colors of nonsense, I find my muse,
It's artful confusion, with no need to choose.

Sails without a Compass

On waves of whimsy, I set my sail,
Adrift in the breeze, where oddities prevail.
The stars are shifty, but shine so bright,
A treasure map drawn in the dark of night.

With each gust of winds, my ship takes flight,
Eating jellybeans instead of slight.
"Where to now?" calls the parrot pariah,
"Follow the giggles and the sweet euphoria!"

Navigating Unseen Terrain

I woke up and spilled my tea,
My cat just stared, judging me.
I tripped on dreams that had no plan,
Yet laughed as if I truly can.

The GPS is lost, so let's just roam,
Following signs that lead us home.
A blindfolded dance on a tightrope,
Delightfully clumsy, a jumbled hope.

I asked my sock where it had been,
It shrugged, and I sensed a grin.
The fridge hums a lullaby so sweet,
As I search for the missing meat.

A dish of chaos on my plate,
Serving up life's absurd fate.
With laughter as my trusty guide,
I bounce on waves, never to hide.

The Art of the Undefined

A canvas blank, yet colors spill,
They dance around against my will.
I scribble thoughts, absurd and bold,
In a gallery where laughter's sold.

A recipe for bread gone wrong,
Yeast took a trip and sang a song.
The pie chart of my plans is skewed,
But who needs math when I'm in the mood?

With every misstep, I find delight,
Like juggling eggs in the pale moonlight.
The universe winks, a playful tease,
While I sip my juice, feeling at ease.

In the chaos, I paint my fun,
With every blunder, I see I've won.
Exploring the strange, the undefined,
It's a circus of thoughts, all intertwined.

Chasing the Ghosts of Purpose

I chased a ghost through an empty hall,
Hoping it'd tell me if I should crawl.
It laughed and vanished into the night,
Leaving me pondering my next slight.

The to-do list winks with a cheeky air,
It knows my plans are quite a scare.
As errands dance like fireflies,
I grin at fate in its disguise.

A sock puppet says, 'Why not just play?'
As I wander off, my mind in disarray.
It suggests a nap over the route,
Why chase a dream that's just a flout?

I crown my thoughts with jester's glee,
In a kingdom where I dare to be.
With silly whims and laughter grand,
I chase my ghost in a whimsical land.

The Mystery of the Unseen Path

I took a step without a clue,
The ground was there, or was it blue?
I laugh and dance in my own head,
While pondering where the socks are led.

With every twist and every turn,
I find new joys and truths to learn.
A chicken crossed, or was it wise?
It winked at me with playful eyes.

Heartbeats in the Void

My heartbeats bounce like rubber balls,
In empty rooms with echoing calls.
What's that noise? Oh, just a sneeze,
I chuckle softly, feeling at ease.

Each breath I take, a comic fate,
Like shadows dancing, and I debate.
If life's a joke, let's share a laugh,
And ride the waves of this wild path.

Echoes of the Unexplained

In the hall, strange echoes arise,
Were those my thoughts or just the flies?
A cat yawned wide, and so did I,
As mysteries floated and waved goodbye.

With every puzzle, I grin and sigh,
Wearing mismatched socks, oh me, oh my!
I stumble through oddities galore,
And wonder what I'm waiting for.

Wandering Through Mists

Walking through clouds, I swing and sway,
Where am I going? Who's to say?
I slip on a banana peel with glee,
Laughing at fate as it laughs at me.

I dance with fog and twirl around,
Chasing whispers without a sound.
In this goofy maze, I spin and prance,
Ignoring the world and its stern stance.

Chasing Fleeting Moments

I chased a bubble in the sky,
It danced like it was oh-so-high.
I tripped on thoughts, fell headlong too,
Now I can't remember why I flew.

My socks don't match, and that's okay,
They giggle at my clumsy sway.
A squirrel chattered, 'What's the fuss?'
I shrugged and then just laughed at us.

A donut rolled across the floor,
I pondered if I should chase it more.
In sticky sunlight, time, it slips,
Like honey on my toast, it drips.

So here I stand, quite out of phase,
In a world of whims and silly ways.
The questions float like cotton candy,
And life, my friend, is just so dandy!

A Maze of Wonder

In a maze of jellybeans I roam,
Singing silly songs, I've found my home.
Walls of marshmallow, twists and bends,
Who needs a map when laughter sends?

A pickle danced, a carrot spun,
I joined the dance, I joined the fun.
The guide was lost—what could he say?
I giggled at the silly day.

Oodles of spaghetti in a bowl,
Making shapes of a lost soul.
A noodle whispered, 'Join the feast!'
I laughed and said, 'I'm quite the beast!'

So let's forget the why and how,
And jump into the silly now.
In this maze where giggles play,
Who needs a reason anyway?

The Language of the Unsaid

With eyebrows raised and eyes so wide,
I read the silence like a guide.
A couch potato told a tale,
While munching chips from an old pail.

We danced around unspoken dreams,
In the sunlight, where laughter beams.
A cat meowed as if to say,
'Why worry 'bout tomorrow's play?'

A sock went missing, so we guessed,
About its journey, a wild quest.
A treasure hunt in laundry land,
Where voices linger, hand in hand.

So join this riddle, face the unknown,
With giggles thrown, and seeds we've sown.
In the joy of not quite clear,
We find our truth, so mad and dear!

Breathless in the Unknown

I stood before a pie of green,
The strangest sight I've ever seen.
A fork appeared with quite a grin,
It said, 'Come taste, just dive right in!'

I sailed on boats of chocolate dreams,
Lost in a world that's bursting at the seams.
A goldfish winked as if to say,
'Just float along, make every day!'

The clocks all melted in the sun,
Tick-tock? Nah, let's just have fun.
I jumped on clouds—goodness, where?
With giggles floating through the air!

So here's my cheer for the unknown,
In quirky paths, we've brightly grown.
With each odd twist, we laugh and spin,
What's clear at heart? The fun we're in!

Relics of Unanswered Longing

I bought a donut for my soul,
It vanished, but I'm still whole.
The universe plays peek-a-boo,
And leaves me guessing what to do.

I wore mismatched socks to work,
Claimed I was a fashion jerk.
But in this chaos, I feel free,
Like a cat that drank too much tea.

The stars are winking, oh so bright,
But their secrets are out of sight.
I shake my head with sheer delight,
Perhaps they just love to incite!

In quest of answers I won't find,
I laugh and dance, I'm undefined.
A box of chocolates, life's parade,
With flavors strange that leave me swayed.

The Beauty of Ambiguity

A pickle in a jar, so green,
Staring at me, quite obscene.
It never tells me what it thinks,
But I can tell it loves my brinks.

Here's a sock that's lost its mate,
With dreams of being fashionable fate.
I wear it on my head in glee,
Where else would it get to be?

Questions hang like misty clouds,
In gatherings, I wear my shrouds.
I drop my phone but it feels grand,
Perhaps it wanted to make a stand.

Life's a riddle, not a rule,
Wobbling like a dingy stool.
I nod to chaos with a grin,
Turns out, it's where fun begins!

Pulses of the Invisible

The fish didn't see me at the park,
Tried to throw bread, but missed the mark.
They swam off, maybe to a club,
Where humans are the real grub.

I once found logic in a shoe,
Told it tales that were simply askew.
It didn't reply; maybe it's shy,
Leaving me with a fumbled sigh.

The weather forecast called for joy,
But landed me a wind-up toy.
I cranked it up and danced away,
Grateful for the silliness on display.

In shadows lurk the 'what-ifs' bright,
I chase them with a heart of light.
In every hiccup, laugh with flair,
You never know what'll be out there!

The Quest for Gentle Certainties

A bubble floated past my door,
It popped and left me wanting more.
A mystery wrapped in swirly fun,
Why's it gone? I had just begun!

I brewed some coffee, thought it wise,
But ended up with muddy surprises.
Who knew the grounds could hold such schemes,
It brewed a dance within my dreams!

In the land of squirrels and trees,
I asked a raccoon for degrees.
He shrugged and said with furry pride,
'You can't spell 'happy' without a ride!'

Wander onward with quirks in mind,
In every twist, a laugh to find.
Certainties waltz with laughs galore,
As life's a party we all adore!

Unfolding in the Twilight

Twilight whispers in my ear,
Where's my sock? It disappears!
I chase the shadows, trip and fall,
The moon just laughs, it sees it all.

Cats are plotting in the trees,
While I search for a lost car key.
The stars are winking, quite a show,
But why they shine, I do not know.

At dinner, spaghetti flies around,
Someone sneezes, chaos found.
I question, why the fork's not here?
It's just a meal but brings such fear!

Yet as I dance through this odd night,
I laugh and shake with sheer delight.
For in this maze, absurd and bright,
The joy of not knowing feels just right!

Open Eyes, Closed Doors

I knock and find the world is odd,
A sign reads 'Welcome, No One's Here!'
Open eyes, but where's my guide?
I wander in, my clueless stride.

Pigeons plot on power lines,
They gossip 'bout the silly signs.
I ask them for a map or clue,
Instead, they coo and just say 'Boo!'

A door swings wide, but then it creaks,
Behind it lies a box of freaks.
I try to laugh, though I might cry,
What game is this? I can't deny!

So I'll embrace this quirky quest,
With grins and giggles, I'll invest.
For in this dance of locked-up dreams,
The fun is in the baffling schemes!

The Curious Dance of the Undecided

I wander here, I wander there,
With mismatched shoes and wild hair.
Should I leap or should I crawl?
The world just spins, I can't recall.

What's for dinner? Oh, surprise!
I find a shoe that's lost its size.
Each decision feels so tough,
But the laughter, oh, that's enough!

I step on toes, I trip on fate,
In this goofy, fleeting state.
Why wear shoes when socks will do?
The handy dandy socks say "woo!"

So I twirl, confused, and spin about,
In this curious dance, there's no doubt.
It's silly to fret on what's ahead,
When giggles bloom, and worries spread!

A Tapestry of Unknowing

Threads of life weave in a mess,
Stitching joy with a touch of stress.
I laugh at patterns, wild and free,
Who knew a sock could come from me?

Each color clashes, spins and twirls,
Making fabric from swirls and curls.
I squint at bright, confusing hue,
It's like a clown went all askew!

Maps are drawn with crayon and flair,
'Adventure here'—oh, look, a bear!
I want to run, but here I stand,
Where's my path? Oh, isn't it grand?

A tapestry so quirky and bright,
I wrap it 'round me, holding tight.
For each lost step and silly spin,
Is a thread of laughter woven in!

The Rhythm of Nonchalance

I dance in shoes of mismatched pairs,
With socks that wave like silly flares.
The world spins round, I just don't care,
In the circus of life, I'm a silent dare.

My alarm clock laughs, it never chimes,
I snooze through each of life's funny crimes.
The cat plays poker with dust bunny climes,
While I sip tea and scribble my rhymes.

Each fruit's a riddle, a funny blind date,
The mango's sweet, but I've missed the plate.
Shall I peel it now, or just contemplate?
In the kitchen of chaos, I'm never too late.

Why chase the rabbit, why seek the moon?
I'll juggle lemons and sing a tune.
Life is absurd, it's a wacky cartoon,
So here's to the joy, and to being a buffoon!

Fleeting Flickers of Insight

I had a thought, but it slipped away,
Like a squirrel on caffeine, too quick to stay.
I chase it down, but it's gone astray,
Leaving me giggling at my own dismay.

What's the meaning of that soup I made?
Was it comfort food or a masquerade?
With every spoon, my doubts cascade,
But I'll laugh it off; I've got jokes to trade.

The light bulb flickers, a disco ball,
Illuminating thoughts that rise and fall.
I grin like a toddler at a spaghetti stall,
Is this wisdom or just a wall?

I ponder deeply like a wannabe sage,
With insights that dance like a furry mage.
Each grand idea is just a new page,
In the book of life's wacky, fun stage!

A Journey Without a Map

I hit the road with mismatched shoes,
Trip over curbs, but I never lose.
Direction? Nah, I just follow clues,
Like lost socks searching for their views.

The GPS says, "What? I can't compute!"
While I stop for ice cream — what a hoot!
Each twist and turn's like a silly flute,
Playing a tune that's totally mute.

In a car full of giggles and odd-shaped snacks,
I navigate life with a box of knick-knacks.
A treasure hunt's on, no time to relax,
Maps are for grown-ups; I'm avoiding the tracks.

So here's to the journey, each stop is a ball,
With no itinerary, we'll weigh no haul.
I'll roll with the punches, I'll never crawl,
In this wild road trip, we'll give it our all!

Serene Unrest

In a hammock swaying, I wonder and sway,
Is this bliss or just a holiday?
With naps as my job, come what may,
I chuckle at chaos in the sun's warm ray.

The clock ticks loudly, what's time anyway?
It's just a suggestion, a game we play.
With coffee in hand, I'm okay with delay,
While the world rushes by in a frantic ballet.

I'll float like a jellyfish, dodging the waves,
In a sea of confusion, I'm not one who braves.
With every "why" that the universe saves,
I snicker and laugh, as a calmness paves.

Life's a puzzle without a clear frame,
But I'll dance through the pieces, no need for fame.
With whimsy as armor, I'm never the same,
In the serene unrest, I'm playing my game!

Darkened Corners of Clarity

In a room where dust bunnies thrive,
I ponder why I'm so alive.
The toaster blinks, my coffee's cold,
Yet here I am, no answers unfold.

Shadows laugh in the dark, quite sly,
As I chase the echo of a pie in the sky.
The clock ticks loud, the cat makes a leap,
I scribble nonsense, drowning in sleep.

A sock is missing, the fridge is bare,
I can't find meaning amidst this despair.
But laughter bubbles like a fizzy drink,
In this crazy circus, I just can't think.

Yet, here I dance, with jelly on toast,
Making toast to the things I love the most.
With each clumsy step, the world tilts wide,
In darkened corners, absurd joys abide.

Horizons Beyond Our Reach

The horizon smiles, a trickster's grin,
Whispers of wisdom, where to begin?
I chase my thoughts on a runaway train,
While pigeons coo, calling me insane.

With spaghetti in hand, I ask the moon,
Why is it always a mystery tune?
A marathon jog through fields of doubt,
I'm out of shape, but I sing loud about.

Clouds morph into shapes that tease my eye,
Is that a dragon or a slice of pie?
A waltz with confusion, so pure and clear,
In this dance of chaos, I hold nothing dear.

Horizons flicker like a faulty light,
I'll run a marathon, while ghosts take flight.
With laughter as my guide along the path,
I embrace the weirdness, and savor the laugh.

Embracing the Unfamiliar

In a world where banana peels slide,
I stumble along, with my panda guide.
The bushes whisper secrets, oh so sly,
As squirrels debate the shape of the sky.

Cards flop under the weight of my glee,
While jellybeans ponder, who could they be?
I wear mismatched socks, a badge of my pride,
In this circus of life, I dance and I glide.

The unfamiliar is sweet like cotton candy,
I swing with the rhythms, feeling quite dandy.
My thoughts jiggle like jelly in a bowl,
In this world of whimsy, I take a stroll.

With giggles and winks, I greet the odd,
Each quirk a layer of life's mighty facade.
Embracing the strange in every nook,
I pen my adventures in a purple book.

Whirlwinds of Indifference

I twirl in my chair, lost in the spin,
The world looks back with a cheeky grin.
Chasing my thoughts like ducks in a row,
While the rain keeps falling, oh what a show!

The fridge hums a tune I've yet to know,
As I search for snacks in the fridge's glow.
A dust cloud marches, bold and spry,
While I muse on "What, when, and why?"

Indifference dances on a thin string,
While I juggle lemons, and begin to sing.
The cat stares blankly, judging my moves,
As I do the hokey-pokey with nothing to prove.

Whirlwinds blow, mixing chaos and cheer,
I spin with laughter, for naught do I fear.
In the carnival of thought where nonsense thrives,
I celebrate the art of absurd lives.

Chasing Shadows of Meaning

In a world of little clues,
I wear mismatched shoes.
I dance like no one sees,
A master of the freeze.

My thoughts are like balloons,
Floating to silly tunes.
I trip on my own rhyme,
But laugh, it's just my time.

I ponder if I'm wise,
While eating pumpkin pies.
The answers hide and seek,
As I just laugh and speak.

Why is the cat so sly?
It jumps, I just ask why.
Embracing fun confounds,
In this game of lost grounds.

Fragments of a Half-Remembered Tale

Once upon a time, they say,
I lost my way today.
With socks that never match,
I set the perfect catch.

I met a cat named Lou,
Who claimed to know the truth.
He rolled his eyes at fate,
And said, 'I'm never late!'

He whispered of a dance,
That left me in a trance.
With twirls and goofy spins,
I wondered where this begins.

Yet as the story flows,
The punchline no one knows.
I chuckle at the jest,
Embracing life's weird quest.

The Drift of Uncharted Winds

I rode a breeze today,
A bird that lost its way.
With feathers made of cheese,
It giggled in the breeze.

With thoughts that slip and slide,
I'm on this wobbly ride.
Navigating strange seas,
In search of smarter bees.

They buzzed about with glee,
Discussing life's mystery.
But I just watched in awe,
As they hummed out the law.

I laughed at windy ways,
In this circus of days.
With every gust that swirls,
I embrace the silly worlds.

Notes from the Edge of Understanding

Jotting down my thoughts,
In the land of doodled knots.
With each squiggle I trace,
I'm finding my own grace.

The sky once told a joke,
But the punchline went up smoke.
I scribble down my fails,
While dreaming of sea gales.

The fridge hums a tune,
As I dance with the moon.
With snacks as my witness,
I laugh at my own fitness.

As secrets hide in plain,
I chuckle through the rain.
These notes weave laughter bright,
In the dark of the night.

Traces of the Unfamiliar

In a world where socks disappear,
I ponder the fate of my missing gear.
Left, right, up, or down, I can't say,
But perhaps they just chose to run away.

The toaster winks, it has a plan,
To set my bread on a crispy tan.
But why's the coffee singing it a tune?
I just wanted breakfast, not a monsoon.

The fridge laughs loud, its door swings wide,
Claiming midnight snacks should not abide.
Yet here I stand, feeling quite bizarre,
With pancakes flying from my cupboard jar.

So here I wander, wrapped in my thoughts,
Chasing lost shoelaces — a bit of fun, not knots.
Life's a game that no one can decode,
Maybe it's best just to dance on the road.

Serenity Amidst the Unknown

A cat on a roof plays hide and seek,
While I'm scratching my head, feeling weak.
The grass whispers secrets, but I can't hear,
I guess I've upset the invisible deer.

The clouds march by with a knowing grin,
Sipping on rain as they sway and spin.
I wave at the sun, it sticks out its tongue,
What's wrong with me? I must be quite young.

My goldfish stares as if it knows all,
When it swims in circles, it gives a call.
Is it laughing? Or just feeling shy?
I'd ask it, but I don't think fish can comply.

So here I float, on a quest so grand,
Chasing wild ducks and a jigsaw band.
Each twist and turn, a giggle or two,
Life's a parade and I'm in the queue.

The Silence of Undefined Dreams

In a land where spoons can suddenly fly,
I chase my imagination, oh my! Oh my!
The clouds wear hats made of cotton candy,
While I trip on thoughts, feeling all dandy.

A dog in a bowtie starts to recite,
Poems of hamsters that twinkle at night.
Is this a circus? Perhaps a charade,
Where giggles are gold and worries do fade.

Naps on a ferris wheel spin me around,
Chasing the echoes of joy that I've found.
But where does the fun keep sneaking away?
It's hiding in laughter; that's what I say!

What gives? I ask as I dance with my shoes,
While my imagination sings a tune of the blues.
I've not a clue, yet still feel so bright,
In this silence of dreams, every wrong feels right.

Distant Drums of Devotion

An elephant plays the trumpet in town,
Hastily puffing, with a comical frown.
The grasshoppers join in a zany parade,
Making rhythms that none can evade.

I juggle my worries like balls made of glee,
Hoping they won't land too close to me.
The frogs in the pond croak a great song,
But are they right or just going along?

A snail in a tux says, "Dress to impress!"
While I stand here feeling quite a mess.
Should I don a hat or perhaps a fine coat?
These choices tie up like a slippery boat.

So onward I bounce, through laughter and cheer,
While the distant drums tell me not to fear.
In the chaos of life, there's a whimsical beat,
Perhaps it's a tune we're all meant to meet.

Uncharted Waters

Sailing through a sea of haze,
Chasing waves in a heated daze.
The compass spins, we laugh and squeal,
While fish throw parties beneath the keel.

The map is blank, not a clue in sight,
Sharks in tuxedos, what a delight!
With every splash, our worries float,
Sunburned noses on a silly boat.

Maybe we're jesters, dressed to impress,
In this circus of life, we dance and guess.
The horizon tips, we might just glide,
Hope sails high on a giddy tide.

Reflections in Serendipity

Mirrors catch giggles on a whim,
Where shadows play hide and seek on a limb.
Each turn reveals a twist of fate,
With every stumble, we celebrate.

Puddles laugh back, splashing me true,
A dance with ducks as they quack 'adoo!'
Bubbles of fortune float by our side,
In the joy of chaos, we take our ride.

A riddle unfolds with a chuckle so bold,
As jigsaw pieces refuse to be told.
With mismatched socks and a crop-top grin,
We navigate whims, where ducklings swim.

A Symphony of Doubt

An orchestra hums of uncertainty,
With violins playing a tune of absurdity.
The conductor sneezes, we all look around,
As the trumpets echo a nonsensical sound.

In between notes, our laughter erupts,
While flutes trip over as the piano interrupts.
This grand performance might end in a crash,
Yet still we waltz, embracing the brash.

With every wrong note, we clap and cheer,
For a symphony built on delightful fear.
No sheet music here, just pure whimsy,
We dance like it's scripted in perfect clumsiness.

Between Questions and Stars

Stargazing wonders with frowns and grins,
Counting what's lost, where nonsense begins.
A constellation beams, but who's in charge?
Is that a rabbit or a giant barge?

Questions twirl in the cosmic cheer,
While comets joke from far and near.
Each twinkle winks at my puzzled face,
In this galaxy of giggles, I find my place.

Galactic clowns in a vast ballet,
Twirling through whispers of what to say.
Between constellations, we lose the thread,
But laughter shades the thoughts in my head.

Questions in the Silence

Why does my cat stare at the wall?
Is there a party I don't recall?
The fridge hums a happy tune,
Yet I'm wondering where's my spoon?

Why do socks vanish in the wash?
Was there a sock thief? Oh, what a posh!
The toaster pops like it's alive,
Yet my poor toast seems to barely survive.

Why do we talk to ourselves so loud?
As if we're some big, important crowd?
Echoes laugh from the empty chair,
I nod and smile, pretending to care.

What's the reason for life's little quirks?
Like when the dog hides all my work?
If answers were dollars, I'd be rich,
Instead, I just laugh at this silly glitch.

Driftwood on a Forgotten Shore

There's driftwood floating, looking so lost,
Did it fight the waves, not counting the cost?
It claims to know secrets of tides and sand,
Yet it just floats there; isn't that grand?

Why did the seagull squawk at my hat?
Is it an expert or just a smart brat?
It puffs up its chest like a sailor in pride,
But really, I think it just wants my fries.

Shells whisper softly from the old gray rocks,
But all I hear is the tick of clocks.
They talk of the depths and the mysteries vast,
While I just wonder, how long can it last?

With all these questions clinging like seaweed,
I laugh at the ocean; it plants a weird seed.
Am I just driftwood, bobbing along?
With no map, just vibes, life can feel like a song.

Embracing the Unexplained

Why does the moon hang out at night?
Is it afraid of the sun's bright light?
It sneaks out to shine, sulking alone,
While we chase our tails, like dogs on the phone.

The coffee machine gurgles its woes,
Yet I can't tell you where my left shoe goes.
Mysterious forces, unseen and shy,
Turn my morning grind into a pie in the sky.

Pants seem to grow legs when they're washed,
Running away when I'm feeling very posh.
Why do we giggle at gravity's call?
The universe chuckles; that's the best part of all.

Perhaps I should dance with confusion so bright,
Twirl with the questions that take flight.
In this wild waltz, where the answers are few,
I embrace the unknown with a joyful "woohoo!".

The Dance of Solitude

In my room, I twirl with the dust in the air,
Dancing with echoes, not a single soul there.
The shadows applaud my whimsical moves,
As I laugh along; my heart simply grooves.

Why do chairs seem like great old friends?
They listen to every story, no end.
I spin and I swirl in this playful retreat,
Falling over pillows, I'm light on my feet.

My goldfish watches with wide, bulging eyes,
Is it judging my moves, or just full of surprise?
It blows bubbles as if to cheer me on,
While I shake my hips until the break of dawn.

Here in my bubble of silliness bright,
The world outside fades; it's pure delight.
With no rhythm required, I'll dance like a pro,
In the silence I find, I'm still ready to glow.

Waves Against the Unknown

The ocean laughs with giddy waves,
Splashing secrets, misbehaves.
The fish wear hats, they dance around,
While crabs tell jokes without a sound.

A seagull shouts, 'Why so serious?'
As jellyfish float, they seem delirious.
With every splash, a question flows,
But who's got time? No one really knows.

The tides roll in with a silly glee,
As lost sailors ponder, 'Could that be me?'
A turtle hums a goofy tune,
Beneath a puzzled, wandering moon.

And when they ask, 'Why are we here?'
The echo laughs, it's all just cheer.
With sandy toes and salty hair,
The unknown dances—who needs a care?

Notes of a Haphazard Melody

A songbird chirps with curious notes,
Bouncing around like silly boats.
Each tune a riddle, none set in stone,
Yet everyone hums along on their own.

A cat plays piano, quite out of tune,
While mice are raving under the moon.
The rhythm stumbles, but who's to fret?
In this jumbled song, no goals are met.

With xylophones made from candy canes,
And drums that echo with silly refrains.
They dance in circles, spinning around,
As laughter wraps their quirky sound.

And if you ask, 'What's the master plan?'
You'll find a parrot with no clear span.
Just sing along; there's joy in the mess,
In notes that tumble, it's anyone's guess.

Encounters with the Invisible

A ghost tried speaking, but no one listened,
He made balloon animals, but they glistened.
In shadows he prances, a jolly old chap,
While humans just think it's a peculiar nap.

A friendly breeze whispers silly tales,
Of wandering spirits, on moonlit trails.
Yet no one's sure where laughter's from,
Just echoes of giggles, a phantom's drum.

The furniture dances, with horror and glee,
As sock puppets frolic, oh, can't you see?
Invisible friends plotting a scheme,
To bake up a ruckus and add to the dream.

And when you ponder, 'What could they seek?'
The air just giggles, 'Oh, aren't they meek?'
A toast to the lost—come join in the fun,
For every dark corner's got laughter to run.

Fleeting Hues of Ambivalence

Colors collide in a muddled parade,
Where pink meets green, and orange is swayed.
A painter shrugs, then flings his brush,
Creating a mess that makes no fuss.

A polka-dotted cat skips down the lane,
Chasing rainbows that dance in the rain.
With paints that giggle and crayons that leap,
Each stroke a riddle too funny to keep.

And people peek in with curious eyes,
Wondering why all this chaos lies.
Yet the artists beam, with hearts full of cheer,
In a world that's wild, what's wrong, my dear?

So let the hues clash and tradition bend,
In this raucous gallery, you'd have to attend.
For every jab and every sneer,
Is just a brushstroke of joy, my dear!

Beneath the Surface of Silence

In a room full of chatter, I nod my head,
But in my mind, it's a dance with the dead.
They ask me for answers, I laugh and I grin,
While my thoughts swim around like fish out of fin.

The clock ticks away, I chase my own tail,
Trying to grasp what's so rock solid, pale.
With every 'Huh?' and a cheeky smirk,
I dive in the depths where the sun doesn't lurk.

Each question posed feels like a tightrope,
Balancing humor and nonsense with hope.
I ponder the stars, an old shoe's delight,
While tumbleweeds rustle in the dead of the night.

So let's raise a toast to the whispers unknown,
Where silence is louder than any loud phone.
With a wink and a smile, we'll wade through the fog,
In the land of confusion, we're all just a cog.

The Art of Embracing Confusion

Why do socks disappear in the abyss?
No one can tell, and that's fine with this bliss.
I honor their absence with dance parties grand,
While the left one's out getting a sunburned tan.

A chicken walks in, thinks it's late for school,
The punchline is lost, playing by its own rule.
In a world full of quirks, I sling a quick jest,
As my brain throws a party, it's never a guest.

When asked for my thoughts, I'll stammer and flail,
Like a fish on dry land with one flipper set sail.
But laughter is magic, the glue in this mess,
While I juggle my thoughts on a unicycle's quest.

So let's make a canvas with brushes unseen,
With splatters of chaos painting the routine.
For in every confusion, there's art that we find,
Crafting giggles and puzzles that tickle the mind.

Footprints in the Dark

Stumbling through shadows, I trip on my fate,
Each footprint I leave is a comedic crate.
I wander in silence, a mime on parade,
And the echoes of giggles begin to cascade.

With every dark corner, I dodge and I weave,
Like a cat on a leash, what tricks to believe!
I laugh at the cosmos, it laughs back at me,
In a game of hide and seek, we're both not quite free.

The stars wink above, in a snarky display,
As I fumble through riddles, come join the foray!
What's that in my pocket? A cookie, a clue?
Or maybe it's nothing; who really knows too?

So let's tiptoe through laughter, embrace every fall,
With footprints of whimsy, we'll dance through it all.
For in every dark moment, there's joy to be sparked,
As we leap through the fog, leaving trails in the dark.

The Nature of Not Understanding

Woke up this morning with toast in my hair,
Is it a new style, or a breakfast affair?
My cat thinks I'm nuts, with a puzzled meow,
As I strut through the house like a confused cow.

In a world made of puzzles, I'm missing some pieces,
Yet laughter erupts, like never-ending leases.
I contemplate why donuts circle so round,
While my coffee jumps ship, it's nowhere to be found.

I scribble my thoughts on the back of my hand,
Only to wipe them off like a wacky bandstand.
Each question arises like popcorn in oil,
Popping up kernels of nonsense to toil.

Let's toast to the chaos, the giggles, the dare,
For not understanding is beyond compare.
So join in this circus, let laughter take flight,
In the nature of nonsense, we'll find the delight.

The Weight of Unasked Questions

If life were a quiz, I'm failing each day,
Multiple choice, yet I choose my own way.
Questions pile up like laundry in heaps,
With answers that giggle while I try to sleep.

Why does my cactus not really need light?
Is it a ninja or just shy of the bright?
I ponder the fate of the socks that don't match,
Are they off plotting schemes without me to catch?

Coffee and donuts, the mysteries grow,
But I can't explain how my plants all just glow.
I question the cereal; is it a meal?
When marshmallows laugh, do they know how to feel?

Yet here I am, dancing with queries so fine,
Filling my head with this whimsical line.
In the fog of my thoughts, I trip on the truth,
But giggles and snickers can fuel my sweet youth.

Dance of the Questions

Twisting and twirling, the questions parade,
Like a conga line, they never fade.
"Why is my hair doing this crazy thing?"
Once I asked a cat, but it just chose to sing.

Waltzing through life with a skip in my step,
Wondering why I can't quite keep my rep.
Is it the socks that I wear with my shoes?
Or the socks that I lose, while searching for clues?

As the rhythm goes on, I shuffle my fate,
Stumbling on choices, it's never too late.
Can my plants speak French, or is that a joke?
They whisper in leaves, while I sit back and poke.

So I dance with my doubts, let the laughter arise,
With each jolly question, I tease and I prize.
In this ballroom of nonsense, we groove side to side,
For in the chaos of life, we take it in stride.

Shadows of Purpose

Shadows flit by like uninvited guests,
With questions that wiggle, they put me to tests.
Are they here for the party, or lost on their way?
I chuckle and shrug; who am I to say?

Does the toaster get jealous when I cook bread?
Or the fridge when I dance, humming 'that song' in my head?
What giggles inside when I trip on my shoe?
I look for the answers, they vanish like dew.

Did my goldfish just wink, or was it a flash?
Is he judging my snack of popcorn and trash?
Queries gather like cats; they scatter and roam,
And leave me to wonder if I've lost my home.

So here in the shadows, I'll keep up the chase,
With a grin on my face and a dash of grace.
For purpose might hide in the quirkiest place,
In laughter and questions, I find my own space.

Drifting Like Leaves

Like leaves on the wind, we're carried and tossed,
Through giggles and chaos, it's never a loss.
Why do ducks waddle in their funky parade?
Is there a rhyme in the dance that they've made?

In puddles I ponder the ants on their quest,
Are they leading a charge, or just looking for pests?
Why does the sky change colors at night?
Are sunsets just blushes, or is it a fright?

With each curious whirl, I spin in my chair,
As questions drift by on the breath of fresh air.
Do fortune cookies know what they have in store?
Or am I just hungry for answers and more?

Yet floating through life like feathers in flight,
I dive into nonsense, and oh, what a sight!
I laugh at the questions that float all around,
For in chasing the whims, true joy can be found.

Glances in the Abyss

I peeked at the void, it winked back at me,
It said, "What's the fuss? Just let it be!"
I asked it for answers, it rolled its big eyes,
"Life's just a dance, not a test with a prize."

I tripped on my shoes, while the abyss just sighed,
"Quit measuring shadows, come take a ride!"
With every step taken, the ground starts to chuckle,
As if secrets were hiding in each little buckle.

It's wild to imagine one's road mapped in ink,
When the scribbles of fate are more like a wink.
Each turn is a giggle, a puzzling jest,
As I laugh at the chaos, I can't help but jest.

So here's to the laughter, the lighter routes seen,
For giggles in dark must be part of the scheme.
Let's frolic in chaos, no need for a plan,
With a wink at the void, let's run, if we can!

The Unwritten Journey

I packed up my bag with an old rubber duck,
And set out to find, just my luck!
Every step was just silly, I lost track of the time,
While chasms of nonsense did seem to rhyme.

The map was a pancake, the compass was bent,
But each twist and turn was quite heaven-sent!
Who needs all the answers, or routes all laid flat,
When the paths are just giggles, and the trees wear a hat?

I passed by some flowers who told me a joke,
They chuckled so hard that the sun nearly broke.
With laughter resounding, I meandered and swayed,
Each moment a riddle, in my leafy parade.

At the end of the road, they handed me tea,
"Here's life's little wisdom, from you to me!"
I toasted to silence, to paths always stray,
For the ride's just a laugh, come what may!

Lurking Beneath Certainties

Beneath every joke, a truth seems to lie,
With a snicker from doubt, as the certainties fly.
I scoured for answers in a bowl made of soup,
While fish-tales in whispers would giggle and loop.

The laws that we trumpet hold wiggles and glee,
As if knowledge has legs and prefers to be free.
In suits of confusion, it dances in fright,
While I try to catch wisdom, it dodges my sight.

Who needs all the reasons when whimsy can shine?
With a hop and a skip, oh, how fun to unwind!
The answers keep winking, obscured in their veils,
As I ride on the waves with my ship made of snails.

So here's to the riddles, absurdity's charms,
To finding joy hiding in chaos's arms.
For none of it matters, we roam for a while,
In a world full of giggles, let's linger and smile!

Caught in the Between

I'm juggling decisions like apples on strings,
The universe chuckles at the chaos it brings.
One foot in the moment, the other in dreams,
As the dance of uncertainty laughs and redeems.

I stood on a tightrope, wearing polka dot shoes,
The ground gave a wink, and shouted, "Choose!"
But every direction felt just like a whirl,
As the left promised sunshine, the right twirled and swirled.

So let's toast to the pauses and the silly delays,
While time plays its tricks in the most merry ways.
For dancing on pinheads is better than rue,
With laughter my partner, and joy always due.

In the space of the gap, the world feels so light,
As I skip through the shadows and flirt with the night.
So why bother knowing what's lost in the haze?
Let's embrace the absurd, and fill life with praise!

Unraveled Threads of Dawn

Chasing shadows in the light,
Where socks mismatch takes its flight.
Coffee brewed, but tastes like mud,
Jokes are cracked, but not a thud.

With toast that burns, we dance in fate,
Spilling jam, it's never late.
Why the cat insists on spree?
Questions buzz like bumblebee.

Umbrellas opened when it's dry,
Streetlight dances, oh my, oh my!
Pants on backwards? What a sight!
We stumble through the morning light.

Laughter wraps us like a hug,
Life's a song, a funny jug.
With puzzled thoughts, we wear a grin,
In a world where we all spin.

Shadows of Uncertainty

In a café full of chatter,
I sip my tea, watch pigeons scatter.
The waiter comes, I order fries,
He laughs and says, "How bold, surprise!"

Strangers pass with woeful gait,
With hats so tall, they call it fate.
A dog in shades just strolls on by,
While I ponder why my shoes are shy.

Which path to take? The left? The right?
I'll follow clouds and take a flight.
A flyer lands upon my head,
With notes of wisdom, slightly red.

Frogs in ties begin to croak,
Crawling vines decide to poke.
Unraveled truths beneath the sky,
With each odd step, we just comply.

Whispers in the Void

The ceiling fan spins round and round,
While I'm lost not making sound.
Chasing thoughts that slip and slide,
Like socks on floors where secrets hide.

Boasting plans that come to naught,
I wave at dreams, they just forgot.
The fridge hums tunes of its own,
Where leftovers become unknown.

Silly hats and paper boats,
I contemplate the life of goats.
Why do they stare? I'll never know,
Perhaps it's fun to see them go.

In corners where the silence sings,
We dance for joy on puppet strings.
Breathing in the quirky charm,
Life's a riddle, it's quite the balm.

The Heart's Silent Quest

With shoes untied and hat askew,
I skip along, not knowing who.
Riding waves of silly thought,
In puddles of dreams, laughter caught.

The clock ticks slow, its humor grand,
Tickling my thoughts like grains of sand.
A squirrel debates a nut's true worth,
While I contemplate my own birth.

Juggling apples, miss the catch,
In a dance, my hip gets scratched.
Why'd the chicken cross the street?
For all the quirks are oh so sweet!

Through life's twists, I find my way,
With a grin, come what may.
Hearts are light, with stories spun,
In this quest, we laugh and run.

The Ocean of Unanswered Queries

Waves toss about, questions fly,
Fish swim deeper, oh my, oh my!
Sandy shores where thoughts get stuck,
Dancing crabs just don't give a cluck.

Seagulls squawk with puzzled looks,
Each glance is worth a thousand books.
Why does the tide come and go?
Ask the starfish, but they don't know!

Buckets filled with dreams unspent,
Seashell secrets, heaven sent.
Who put the fun in this grand jest?
Even the seaweed takes a rest.

So grab your buoy, let's set sail,
In this ocean, we'll never fail.
Laughing at the void, what a must,
In this sea of questions, we trust!

Breaths of the Unknown

Inhale deep, what's that smell?
A mystery brewed in a wishing well.
Exhale laughter, hiccups galore,
Breathless chaos makes us roar.

Clouds above, do you see 'em dance?
Maybe they're on a silly romance.
Puddles whisper, splashes sing,
The unknown's joy is a curious thing.

Fleeting dreams on wings of air,
Catch them quick, if you dare!
Who knew that joy could be so light?
Like butterflies tickling the night.

With every breath a riddle's spun,
Maybe life's just one big pun.
So take a breath, let it flow,
In the unknown, let your heart glow!

Silent Currents

Whispers drift through the still night,
What's that lurking, oh what a sight?
The shadows giggle, the moon just grins,
Beneath the silence, the ruckus begins.

Rivers trickle, secrets they share,
But we just nod, with vacant stare.
Paddling canoes in our own minds,
Finding humor in what blinds.

Hidden currents, playful and sly,
They tickle our thoughts, oh me, oh my!
The fish wiggle with secrets to tell,
Laughing at us, all is well.

With every ripple, a new joke flows,
We chuckle along as the dark wind blows.
What's the punchline? Who can perceive?
In silent currents, we just believe!

Unraveled Threads

Sweaters fall apart, yarns in a mess,
Knots of confusion, oh what distress!
Mom's old sewing kit has lost its charm,
But tangled laughter works like a balm.

Fuzzy thoughts weave a curious tale,
Each stitch a giggle that won't derail.
Lost in fabric, we twist and shout,
Who knew chaos had such a route?

Buttons pop off, just like our plans,
Hilarity reigns in these yarn-filled hands.
Woolly wonders, tangle it more,
Every loop is a laugh to explore!

So let's embrace these threads undone,
In the fabric of life, we find the fun.
Stitching together all that we find,
With each unravel, new joy aligned!

Traversing a Mystery

Waking up with socks that don't match,
Wondering why my toast always has a catch.
Cats stare like they own the whole scene,
While I trip on dreams that are never quite keen.

My coffee's a puzzle, a riddle in a cup,
It whispers my secrets, then just gives up.
Why do I laugh when I'm all alone?
Guess that's how it feels to talk to your phone.

The sun keeps rising, but what does it mean?
Chasing shadows of a life I haven't seen.
Each day a circus, laugh tracks in the air,
Like walking a tightrope, but I forgot where.

So here I am, with a grin on my face,
Dancing through the maze without any grace.
Following trails of crumbs, oh what a game!
Will I find an answer? I don't even know the name.

The Weight of Unasked Questions

Rubbing my chin in a thoughtful pose,
While my lunch has a mind of its own, it knows.
Why do we giggle at the silliest things?
Maybe it's tied to the joy that it brings.

The cat just rolled over; could it be a sign?
Or is it just lazy, that feline divine?
I ponder the purpose of socks on a chair,
Like where do they go when they simply disappear?

Climbing a mountain of questions unclear,
I trip on a thought, and then I can't steer.
Is laughter a compass? Or just noise in the breeze?
I'll ask Mr. Elephant, sitting under the trees.

Yet here I am, adrift in the fun,
As the sun lazily sets, while we wait for the pun.
With a wink to the universe, I dance to the beat,
Unraveling nonsense, oh what a treat!

Clouds of Uncertainty

Wandering through fluff that doesn't quite rain,
Searching for answers, but all's just a game.
The wind tells a joke, or maybe it's me,
While pondering dinner—what will it be?

Recipes lurking like ghosts in the night,
Pasta or pizza? It's a puzzling flight.
Could broccoli be plotting against my taste?
Or is it just broccoli, that bumpy green waste?

The sky can't decide if it's blue or it's gray,
Like socks in the dryer, they blend all day.
Life's like a crossword with missing squares,
I giggle and wonder, do you see the bears?

So here I float on clouds, having my fun,
With questions like balloons, oh where do they run?
Laughing at logic as ducks start to quack,
In this whimsical world, I won't look back!

Lost in the Labyrinth of Thought

I ventured inside my mind, a twisted maze,
Where left is right, and up is a phase.
Thoughts play hide and seek beneath my brows,
Like cats who've taken on the role of the house.

Maps made of giggles, paths marked by jest,
Trying to find out which quest is best.
Why do we find ourselves asking the sky,
When it's cookies we crave, no need to be sly?

Each door leads to riddles, each turn to a pun,
With giants who shuffle, and snail races run.
I steal a quick glance at a squirrel in a tie,
Suddenly wondering just how and why.

Yet here I am—no hurry, no strife,
Sailing through this labyrinth called life.
With a chuckle, I dance on thoughts that go round,
In this comedy show, laughter's the sound!

www.ingramcontent.com/pod-product-compliance
Lightning Source LLC
Chambersburg PA
CBHW051631160426
43209CB00004B/607